THE WILDER SIDE OF PROVIDENCE

THE WILDER SIDE
OF PROVIDENCE

and other true and false tales

by

MARGARET REINHART

THE GOLDEN QUILL PRESS
Publishers
Francestown   New Hampshire

Library of Congress Catalog Card Number 92-90013

ISBN 0-8233-0479-5

Printed in the United States of America

*Dedicated
to my husband, my childen
and my grandchildren.
They never forget me, either.*

ACKNOWLEDGEMENTS

My special thanks to:

    Dick Emmons for always encouraging

    Pam Shultz for gently persisting

    Dick and Mary Jeanne Lane for ''welcomputering''

    and José Sanchez for constantly remembering

CONTENTS

THE WILDER SIDE OF PROVIDENCE

NOBODY'S PERFECT

Friend or Foliate

During my life span I have probably collected an enemy or two. I have always felt that these so-called antagonists lacked sufficient reason for their animosity toward me, since I am a clean-living, generous and well-meaning person who would never hurt a fly.

In addition to these human forms, I could also include wire coat hangers, cereal boxes, tight jar lids, designer dress patterns and whodunit paperbacks with the last five pages missing. But the greatest of these hostile objects or beings designed to tamper with my temper is the horticultural menace known as the house plant.

In a garden shop the other day I spotted a lovely plant with absolutely stunning large red flowers. Throwing caution out the window, I bought it. As the clerk applied the protective wrapping, I meekly asked the name of this beauty. She gave me a look that reeked of fertilizer and haughtily informed me that I had just purchased a Hawaiian *schizopetalus*. Giving her a what-did-I-ever-do-to-you glance in return, I left, clutching my prize.

Within a week my *schizopetalus* had developed schizophrenia. Having lost contact with its new environment, and having suffered a disintegrated personality, it bade me a sad aloha and took off for that big luau in the sky.

In the past my *dryopteris phegopteris* has dried up, my *cycas revoluta* revolted, and my *denticulata* developed trenchmouth.

11

You probably don't know anyone who:

Owns a Christmas cactus which brings forth one beautiful blossom—in May.

Has a venus fly trap with real teeth? (And the scars to prove it.)

Possesses a mother-in-law's tongue which has taken over the whole house. Figures.

Owns a spider plant that lures flies right into the room.

Has a maidenhair fern with a crew cut.

Well, you do now.

I have tried talking, singing, shouting and even ignoring these botanical beasts, with no result. A foliated, flowering foe is no fun.

Altogether, Now—

One of the things that fills me with terror is being asked to dance. This may sound ridiculous to you, but if, when you were nine years old and your dancing teacher suggested to your mother that her money would be better spent in finger painting lessons for you, you would understand.

As I said, when I have been asked to dance I have learned to politely decline, saying truthfully that I simply don't know how. This discourages no man. Somehow he had convinced himself that I am another Ginger Rogers, and he persists. Sighing, I reluctantly agree to dance, only to suffer the humiliation later of not being asked out onto the floor again. All of this is due to my tragic lack of coordination which has plagued me throughout my life.

I would like to say that this infirmity ends here. Wrong. Having bowled more balls into the gutter than down the alley, having struck out in every baseball game and having seen more of my golf balls disappear into the woods than land on the fairway, I must extend this ineptness to include athletic endeavors. Let's face it, **a klutz is a klutz**.

The word coordination takes on a different aspect when it refers to one's wardrobe. It is not unusual for me to buy a beautifully designed pair of black shoes only to remember on my way home that I have nothing in my closet to "go with" them. Logic would tell me to return the shoes, but pride does not allow me to admit my mistake and I venture out again to find a black dress to "go with" them. My credit card is fraying at the edges. I have learned, to my regret, that there is a difference between sunshine yellow and lemon yellow, baby pink and raspberry pink and moss green and apple green. I could wish I were colorblind, but it would only tell me who my real friends are, without asking.

But why stop here? Our home is full of furniture and other items ranging from Early American to Colonial to Victorian to Contemporary to, of all things, Mexican. Our refrigerator, range, sink and dishwasher were all avocado. For once I thought I did it right. Now, anything replacing these items must be in another color, since avocado went out with the Middle Ages. Our dishwasher is now Avocado Black.

It would be nice if I could mention something here about rouge, lipstick, nail polish and eye shadow, which I am forced to regard as "matchless," but I must at this time put dinner on the table. This meat is ready to serve, however the vegetable seems to be slightly over cooked. Now all I have to do is wait for the potatoes that can't tell time. Even in the kitchen I can see my unregulated life passing before my eyes, and I sigh.

Convention Trips I Never Should Have Taken

Trip #1—Kansas City, Missouri—Regional

Preparing for the trip, I waltzed around the bedroom in my new black cocktail dress, smirking. "Wait until the other wives see me in this! They will put their husbands on leashes at the banquet."

Result: It wasn't a banquet. It was the K-C Ranch's famous barbecue, and all the women wore jeans and a plaid shirt. Have you ever tried eating barbecued ribs in a black lace dress? Sitting on a horse?

Trip #2—St. Louis, Missouri—Regional

Packing my jeans and plaid shirt I was determined to do it right this time. If those Missouri people like barbecues, I'm ready for them.

Result: It wasn't a barbecue. It was a backyard buffet at the home of the Mayor, and I was the only woman there that wasn't wearing a caftan. Hizzoner thought I had crashed the party.

Trip #3—Palm Springs, California—National

I threw in the jeans, the shirt, the caftan, the mink jacket and the cocktail dress. Nobody's going to fool me again.

Result: It was a lovely pool party and everyone wore guess what the whole time. Occasionally I would catch my husband glaring at me for spending next month's mortgage payment on the new swim suit which I had to buy in a hurry from the hotel boutique.

Trip #4—Miami, Florida—National

Now that I was in full control of the clothing department I thought I would try to look glamorous no matter what I wore. So I asked my beautician to install some false eyelashes for that provocative look.

Result: The first afternoon out I applied plenty of suntan oil to my face, keeping away from the eyes. However, one jump in the pool relieved me of six lashes on one lid and seven on the other.

Trip #5—New Orleans, Louisiana—Regional

Okay. Forget the eyelashes and settle for a facial to give me a fresh, relaxed look, and maybe get rid of the hair above my upper lip.

Result: Hair over upper lip is gone, along with two layers of skin. I tried to compensate by telling everyone that the "in" people were wearing rouge in that spot this year. It was either that or a fake moustache.

Trip #6—London, England—International

I think I'll just settle for a new permanent and a rinse. Everything else I plan seems to go the wrong way. Now I'll be able to really enjoy myself and not worry, at least about my hair.

Result: Now I know why the Englishman always carries an umbrella. Because it rains, that's why. I thought it was because he didn't know what to do with his hands. Yesterday some woman pointed me out to her friend, saying, "Isn't that Phyllis Diller with a new orange wig?" A pox on all hairdressers.

Trip #7—Houston, Texas—National

That's where my husband is going—Houston. Me? I am going to Phoenix, to Madame Cleo's. There I'll be wearing nothing but a leotard. They will exercise me, diet me, massage me, wax me, sauna and steam me, fix my make-up, my hair and my nails. In other words I am going in like Zasu Pitts and coming out like Faye Dunaway. What can possibly go wrong?

I (Can't Even) Remember Mama

One of the dastardly whims of Fate which afflicts those of us who are no longer members of the "younger set" is the disease known as *ipso facto memoranda*, wherein the afflicted can remember clearly what happened on April 10, 28 years ago, but cannot recall what happened last week.

This approach to senior citizenry is no more strongly felt than at the growing realization that to remember a name and attach it to a face or figure is the most frustrating of all social encounters. This malady can sometimes occur earlier in large families, where the mother had literally completed a roll call of her children before she finally attached the right name to the face she faced.

The watergate cover-up is nothing compared to the excuses which have been used for such lapses of memory many of us experience, to our chagrin. I have listed a few of these little alibis here for those of you who wish to avail themselves of an escape from this sort of tight situation. It is suggested, however, that you do not attempt to utilize them until after you are retold the name of the one you are introduced to for the second, or third, or tenth time.

This new medication I am taking has made me so forgetful.

With luck you will be speaking to a sympathetic person who will forgive you immediately and even inquire as to the present state of your health, giving you the opportunity to elaborate on your devastating illness, at the same time easing your conscience. The fact that you were

16

seen a week ago whooping it up at a local discotheque by this same person is a thousand to one shot, but it's the chance you have to take.

I could have sworn you were Anne Bancroft.

Flattery goes a long way, but if the addressee looks more like a female version of Karl Malden, you will have to come up with another excuse—and fast!

You look so different from the way I remember you.

This statement is a lot safer than you might think. The person addressed will of course wonder how he or she looks different, even though nothing has changed in the last 10 years, so while your victim ponders this mystery, you deftly change the subject.

Dear me, how could I have forgotten someone who dresses so beautifully?

You do not make this response to someone who is wearing orange slacks, a purple blouse, red shoes, and carrying a green sweater. There are limits to this wily remark, so act accordingly.

I knew your name was Mary, but I keep wanting to call you Alice—isn't that ridiculous?

It certainly is, but it may work when everything else has failed, and you have descended to the bottom of the list of workable ploys.

Keep these suggestions in mind, and do try to avoid the following:

Your attempt	*Probability*
You've lost weight, haven't you?	2 lbs.
You're wearing your hair differently?	Missed hair appointment
How are the children?	Childless
How is your husband?	Deceased
It's been such a long time.	Yesterday
Where have you been keeping yourself?	Right here

If ever the world wished to forgive one group of people on this earth for its iniquities, let this experession of mercy be bestowed upon those of us with failing memory so that our tombstones can proudly carry this profound epitaph:

You forgave—but I forgot.

No, I Am Not Getting Old!

The other day I asked my son what he would think of my getting a face lift. He replied, "At your age you're supposed to have wrinkles."

Very funny. Just because a woman has wrinkles only a fortune teller could read can only mean she knows almost all the answers. All one has to do is ask the questions, and I wish someone would, just once.

Another thing—gray hair. Just because two of my children have a touch of gray in their hair it only means that they probably have inherited my white-haired husband's genes, not mine.

Besides, I still have an eye for a handsome man with good looking legs. There are a few faces stashed away in my memory, but even today I don't mind at all if today's hunk helps me across the street. I'm not dead yet, you know.

Also, everybody likes to relax once in a while. Even though my favorite place is my rocking chair, I tell myself that I never did like to rock it anyway. Besides, it's easier on my back especially after a hard day driving my cart around the golf course. As you can see, I am not house bound yet. I've even joined a health club and one of these days I'm really going to show up there.

Furthermore, I can only snicker when some young thing asks "Who's Rudolph Valentino?" or "Tyrone who?'' Too bad they can't keep up with things. All they can talk about is Madonna, whoever she is.

And what's so terrible about wearing bifocals? I've had them since I was thirty, which hasn't been too long ago, and besides, they're something you can get attached to, like a dog, or a canary. Not only that, I have removed all my medicine from the medicine cabinet and moved them to the linen closet shelf. It makes the labels easier to read since they are now at eye level.

It's too bad women have to be teased about reading the obituaries in the daily papers. How were you going to express your condolences to your friend if you hadn't noticed the passing of her beloved 90-year-old aunt? Only recently I noted the demise of a much older cousin I hadn't seen in years. Calling it luck would be an improper word.

Lastly, I just can't stand, and have no patience with people who are intolerant. They seldom know what they are talking about and I strongly object to their opinions in the first place.

So don't look at my wrinkles and tell me I'm getting old. I haven't even begun to procrastinate yet.

FOREIGN WORDS AND PHASES

When in Rome

It can sometimes be said, to our shame, that we who love to travel to other countries can speak no other language than English, if indeed that is what we think we have mastered. Consequently we tend to frequent places in those countries where we can be sure of communicating with someone who understands us when we complain about not receiving all the comforts of home, or about the lack of a good hamburger or fries or of the absence of ice in our drinks!

Since it will be ever thus, and even though it may be a small contribution toward educating the traveler, I want to acquaint you with just a few expressions you may wish to be aware of should you hear them spoken in, let us say, the country of France, where a Frenchman will occasionally voice his opinion in his native tongue.

The French do not look favorably on the visitor who has not learned their language, and as a result of this attitude some of these remarks, but not all, of course, will tend to affect your sensibilities. In translating a few of these expressions I can only suggest that when you hear them you counter them with a smile or a shrug of your shoulders. *Bourgeoisie*—This means you are of the working class, just a shade above a peasant or a rube. *Vin Ordinaire*—An anonymous table wine, usually ordered by the *bourgeoisie*, to the disgust of the wine steward. *Sacrebleu!*—This is sometimes uttered by someone who has been insulted by your meager tip. *Chacun a son gout*—Whatever turns you on. You can be sure this is something your modiste would not wear to a dog fight. *Qui tondrait sur un oeuf*—Hard to translate, but roughly means they don't make them any stingier than you. *Qui se mouche trop son nez en tire du sang*—There are a lot of words here, but generally speaking it says "One more peep out of you and we will ship you home on the next plane." A tour guide's final warning. *Se mettre dans le queule du loup*—The cab driver will take you there but you are taking your life in your hands, whatever that means. You may have to walk back to your hotel. *Chambres a louer dans la tete*—This means you have a hole in your head. *Tant pis*—Tough rocks, kiddo. *C'est la mer a boire*—This means you are trying to drink all the wine in France at one sitting, you idiot! *Chien de l'enfer*—Whatever you've done, you're in trouble now, baby. *Demander de la laine a un ane*—You can't get blood from a stone, so there's no use asking for a taco in a French restaurant. *Merde!*—any four letter word. *La vie de boheme*—How they regard the camera toting, guide book carrying, loud shirt wearing tourist.

In spite of all this animosity, you will be enchanted with France, with Paris, with the countryside, the Loire valley and the chateau country, with the Louvre, the Arc de Triomphe, Versailles and so much more. *C'est vrai, n'est-ce pas?*—It's true, isn't it? *Oui, c'est ca.*—Yep, that's the way it is.

The Heart of Mexico

Whenever I hear anyone speak about traveling in another country and being at the mercy of ill-mannered natives, or warn of the possibilities of being robbed or mugged someplace away from home, I always remember an incident involving myself and my husband on a warm, sunny afternoon in Mexico City many years ago.

We love Mexico, my husband, Fred, and I. We have visited this country 20 times in as many years, and have found its people friendly, gentle and warm. The children are delightful and as artful as the shop owner in the marketplace who tries to extract from you an amount of money three times the worth of the article he is attempting to sell you. One Mexican lad was unsuccessful in trying to sell Fred a buffalo nickel, but had no difficulty persuading him to allow his sneakers to be shoe-shined by this same boy.

At the time of my story we were staying at the Geneve, a very old and respectable hotel, many of its rooms still furnished with red velvet drapes and heavy Spanish furniture. It was inexpensive, which suited our budget, and was situated on the Calle Londres in the heart of the Pink Zone, an exceptionally good shopping area for tourists. From here one could walk to the Paseo de la Reforma, one of the most beautiful boulevards in the world, and which could take you to the glorious Museum of Anthropology, Chapultepec Castle, or even to the Zocalo, where Moctezuma reigned until the Spaniards came. There is so much to see in this great city that even after 20 years we felt as if we had seen only a small portion of what it offers in Indian and Mexican lore.

Sunday is a big day here for the visitor. You begin in the early morning by shopping at the Thieves Market, then on to the Ballet Folklorico de Mexico, then to the Floating Gardens of Xochimilco, and finally to the bullfights.

On this particular Sunday afternoon, however, we decided to look over the University of Mexico, a splendid example of architectural design and superb Mexican artistry. We walked a few blocks from our hotel to the Avenida Insurgentes, where we boarded a bus heading for the university.

As in many buses you have seen, there was the usual long seat behind the driver which holds three people, and which faces a similar seat across the aisle. We sat behind the driver, Fred in the middle, I on his right, and on his left a man wearing trousers and shirt, and a vest of outdated variety which had a fabric belt and small buckle across the back. Across the aisle from us was a man accompanied by his small son, about six or seven years old, and a middle-aged woman obviously traveling alone.

Suddenly, as we were riding along, I noticed a hand working its way into Fred's right-hand trouser pocket. At the same time Fred jumped and reached for his wallet. The hand immediately retreated and began the pretense of fumbling with the buckle on the back of his vest. We both glared, then, at our seatmate, who looked straight ahead as if nothing had happened. At the next stop, he quickly jumped off the bus. Unknown to us, all this had been observed by the man sitting across the aisle. As soon as the culprit had departed, and before anyone else could claim his seat, he whispered something into the boy's ear. The boy quickly rose, crossed the aisle, seated himself beside Fred, and gave him a reassuring smile. Then we understood. As I looked into the eyes of the boy's father, I could almost read the message of sadness and regret at the treatment we had received, and was moved by his kind effort to protect us from further annoyance.

Only heaven is the perfect place, and very far away. But a guardian angel can be anywhere. We know. This one was on a bus. He was only six or seven years old but he had a proud little heart, and he stayed with us all the way to the university.

The Traveler

He bought a stereo. He was transported on musical wings to the world of melody, aria, and song. He soared with the classics, danced along with the big bands, square-danced his way through Nashville, and shouted, "Bravo!" for the operatic arias from Milan. He was happy. She flew to Acapulco. She swam in the surf, walked the beach, mingled with the crowd and visited the marketplace. She ate tortillas and tacos and enchiladas. She was happy.

He bought a moped. He felt the breeze in his face as he toured the countryside, up hill and down hill. He was exhilarated. She went to Disney World and saw the wonderful world of fantasy and adventure. She cheered with the rest when Mickey Mouse led the parade. She was exhilarated.

He bought a motorcycle. He rode into the wind, filled with excitement. He marveled at the speed with which he could cover the freeways and the cities and towns and friends he would finally be able to see. He was grateful for this opportunity. She saw Spain—and Portugal. She was delighted with the small fishing village of Nazare, the charm of the Alhambra in Granada, the lovely city of Seville, and she marveled at the awesomeness of Philip's El Escorial, and the beauty of the Prado in Madrid, with its works by Goya and El Greco. She was grateful for this opportunity.

He bought a snowmobile. He loved the winter and knew that he could ride where no car could ride and view the gifts of nature which were now covered with a blanket of pure white and breathe where the air was clean and sharp. He felt humble. She traveled to Italy. She rode a gondola through the canals of Venice. In Rome she walked where Caesar walked. In Pompeii, she wandered through the ancient streets and sensed the life that once was there, and in Florence, after seeing Michelangelo's David, she could not speak. She felt humble.

He bought a boat. He rode on big lakes, small lakes, and rivers. He swam and he fished, and with his raft he fought the rapids. He raced with other boats and won. He wept with joy at his good fortune. She went to Greece and cruised the islands. She rode a mule to the top of Santorini, she saw the birthplace of the Minoan civilization, she could almost hear St. Paul speaking in the streets of Ephesus, and she sang to the hills at Delphi. In Athens, she climbed the Acropolis. When she reached the top and gazed at the splendor of the Parthenon, she wept with joy at her good fortune.

He bought a car. He drove through the 48 states, from New England to California, from Miami to Minnesota. He saw Williamsburg, and Gettysburg, and Washington, D.C., Atlanta and New Orleans. He saw Yellowstone, and the Grand Canyon and the Petrified Forest, the Grand Tetons and the Black Hills. He saw the Alamo and San Francisco. He saw the Rockies and the Mississippi and the cornfields of Kansas, and he loved the beauty of this country. She went to England and Holland, Austria, Bavaria and Germany, France and Switzerland. She saw Buckingham Palace and the Changing of the Guards, the Cottswolds, Stonehenge, Oxford University and the British Museum, and oh, the castles and palaces!

He's older now. With his car or his boat or his stereo he's gone where he wanted to go and seen what he wanted to see. And he can do it again. He purchased long-term investments, and he doesn't regret one minute of it.

She's older now. She thinks it is getting late, and there is not enough time for her to do and see everything in this beautiful wide world. She bought the short-term investment, the one-time shot, and even though she could do it only once, she is filled with memories and doesn't regret one minute of it.

What kind of traveler are you?

Sprechen Sie Englisch?

Do you shun escorted tours? Would you like, for once, to be on your own with your own little car and your own little map, with no hotel reservations to force you into being in a certain place at a certain time? And on a budget?

Your problems are over. You have come to the right person, one who will acquaint you with the ins and outs of independent travel. So pick up your suitcases and we'll be on our way.

This past June I traveled with my husband and daughter, Susan, into East and West Germany for a period of twelve days. We landed in Frankfurt, West Germany, picked up our ample sized VW, a four-cylinder number guaranteed to behave nicely on the Autobahn (German for no speed limit). It was embarrassing to be moving along at seventy miles per hour and being forced to drive in the slow lane in order to make way for cars half the size of ours to cruise past us at one hundred ten miles per hour.

We proceeded toward the East German border at Eisenach with our passports, our humble requests for visas and a tear-jerking story about wanting to visit relatives (none of whom were among the living) and then move on to Prague, since rumor had it that you couldn't enter East Germany without a hotel reservation. Our planned dialogue went out the window when we approached the border only to find there was no one there to greet us, quiz us, see our passports, etc. and we simply moved right through the checkpoint. This freedom of passage was contrary to the best official advice we had received with regard to entrance into East Germany.

We made a point of heading for the railroad station and tourist information office in each city we visited, where we were booked into anything from a private home to a posh hotel. In Eisenach we were placed in a lovely private home, given a welcoming beer and of course a nice breakfast, which each night's lodging provided all through the trip. We also learned that there is no German word for "ice," that soap is not provided except in expensive hotels and that toilet paper could be anything from Charmin to Uncle Walt's Butcher Wrap.

Our first day we rode with our young interpreter, Torsten, to the village of Obermahler in an effort to dig up my husband's ancestors (not literally, of course). We were not successful but Torsten will try to send us further information from the record keeper in the village who was absent on the day we were there, naturally.

We then moved on to Erfurt and Weimar, then back across the border into Nuremberg. Since this is not intended to be a travelogue I will only say that we took advantage of sightseeing tours in Munich, Trier and a great one in Nuremberg which we highly recommend. In one of the hotels we were blessed with a TV set. Even though this was not one of our requirements, it was fun to watch Kermit the Frog sounding off in German, as well as cast members in M.A.S.H., the A-Team, Golden Girls, Hart to Hart and L.A. Law.

It was not unusual when visiting a restaurant to have someone else fill the empty chairs at your table. At one we were struggling with a German menu when two men joined us who were speaking to each other in German. Finally I summoned enough courage to ask if either one spoke English. One man replied "Sure. We were just having fun watching you trying to read the menu." Out of the kindness of my heart I allowed him to live, only because this German had a sense of humor.

In Heidelberg there was a convention and we ended up in the worst of our hotel rooms, with a bath down the hall. On my first visit I locked the door with a rusty key, then was unable to unlock it when it came time to leave. It turned out later to be the only bath on the floor with hot water. Don't ask how we managed.

In Nuremberg my husband went to a nearby hotel restaurant bar, told them his wife had injured herself and needed an ice pack. He returned happily carrying a plastic bag containing ice cubes. Oh, happy day!

In Trier, our second last night out we splurged on a fancy hotel within walking distance of all we wanted to see. I mention the hotel only to list for you our choices for breakfast the next morning: 4 kinds cereal, 5 kinds bread plus croissants, 8 kinds meat, 9 kinds cheese, 2 juices, 5 marmalade, 5 jelly, 5 cereal toppings and soft boiled eggs in their cups. Having mastered the art of eating from an egg cup, I was able to behave like a pro, almost to the point of buying some of these cups to take home with me.

We rode the subway in Munich, the bus in Trier and the horse-drawn cart at the King Ludwig II castle in Neuschwanstein. We saw the building where the Nuremberg trials were held, we visited Berchtesgaden and avoided Dachau. We walked a lot, we stayed well and were treated courteously wherever we went. What more could we have asked for, except ice?

FAMILY MATTERINGS

You Haven't Lived Until....

You make pea soup in a pressure cooker and end up mopping it off the ceiling.

You try to apply lipstick as soon as your dentist dismisses you after freezing one half of your face and find yourself with a red lower lip listing toward the dimple on your chin.

You tell your husband to please name your newly born twins and he says "You mean I have to do THAT too?"

You develop acne at age 45.

You surprise your husband on his birthday with a portrait of yourself by one of Ohio's well-known chalk artists and he says he will attach a plaque to it saying "Our Founder" and keep it lit with a votive candle.

You find, while your 2nd Lieutenant husband is in the army, that it's said you can spot a 2nd Louie because he has a convertible, a cocker spaniel and a pregnant wife—and there's no place for you and the dog to hide.

You break into your brand new expensive Cadillac in thirty seconds with a piece of wire after leaving your keys inside by mistake, thanking your stars that the car had remained where you left it.

Your first child is born in Temple, Texas during a snowstorm the city hasn't seen in 50 years. Your husband and car are miles away and no taxi will drive you to the hospital.

You bring home from Greece what you thought was a gallon container of olive oil, only to find (who can read Greek) that you have a gallon of Greek olives, and you hate Greek olives.

At the Par 3 seventh hole your drive is perfect, but your ball lands on the lip of the cup and stays there.

You marry for love, you and your husband have four beautiful and healthy children who treat you with respect and kindness, you have many wonderful friends and life has been more than good to you. Then you know you have lived.

Whatever Turns Me Off

1. In our house we have six rooms and eight radios, one of which is battery operated, and for which I refuse to buy the copper tops, thereby conveying to my husband the fact that there is a limit to my aural endurance.

All of these radios are tuned into the same station, so that if they were all tuned on at the same time someone like Bruce Springsteen could invade our happy home with an impact that would have us surrounded with screaming teenagers outside seeking his autograph.

Now, I don't need this. What I do need is a radio substitute for my noise-pierced ears, like a pair of diamond earrings.

2. Every once in a while the Edison Company, for some reason, switches off our power for a period of anywhere between one second and ten minutes. We are not talking outages here as a result of a storm or a broken transmitter or whatever it's called. These things happen. We are talking about the one second it takes to transform our clocks (all 7 of them) into blinking twelve-o'clock idiots or slow running timepieces. This of course necessitates a tour of the house to set things right. These adjustments are compounded in the Spring and Fall with daylight saving time, when not only the clocks have to be reset (including the one in the car) but the $7.98 digital watches we have on hand, or should I say wrist.

I don't need this. What I do need is a sun dial that operates indoors.

3. There are days when I actually enjoy cooking. New recipes fascinate me, and when I am in the mood I will browse through a magazine or a fancy cookbook for something new. However, every time I come across a tempting dish to add to my culinary repertoire I immediately begin to assemble the necessary ingredients for these recipes, only to find that I am missing balsamic vinegar, Japanese rice wine, porcine mushrooms, Sicilian olives, black sesame seeds, aragula or walnut oil, or something equally devastating.

I don't need this. It's possible for me to acquire these ingredients if I want to drive fifty miles to the nearest specialty store. I'm sure Julia Child or Martha Stewart never heard of Pinckney or they would have taken pity on us poor country folk and would not have expected us to search our brains or cupboards for substitutes. What I really need is a new wall can opener.

At this time I will not go into today's hemlines or the requirements for a complete wardrobe, nor will I dwell

33

on a water softener that conks out and turns my white sheets into brown studies in my washer. And even as I write this and my ballpoint runs out of ink, I look at the bright side, count my blessings, put on my rose-colored eye shades and go back to bed.

Golden Oldies—Or Family Pearls of Wisdom and Remembrance

Overheard: Our 5-year-old daughter saying to her younger sister, "If you don't do what mother says, she'll give you an enema, and they don't taste very good." This from a student who was later accepted at U of M Medical School, but chose instead a ministerial education at Yale Divinity.

My younger daughter lashing out at me, "I'm not going to bring up my children the way you're bringing up yours!" This from a child who wanted twelve children, but on second thought decided to have none at all. Thank goodness!

To my husband I remarked, "It says here in the paper that this ninety-year-old man is still going to the office every day. Will you still be going to your office when you are ninety?" His reply: "If I am, watch out when I get home!"

Chastising our 4-year-old daughter we asked, "You didn't do this to your little sister, did you?" Her reply: "I didn't?"

Life's little mysteries. Leaving our four at home while we attended a New Year's Eve party and arriving home finding everyone still alive and safe. But how and why was the toilet seat broken? We'll never know.

Our older daughter, now driving, backing into the minister's car in the church parking lot. Saints preserve us!

Our twin son pouring sand into the oil delivery pipe leading into our furnace. His twin brother poking a large nail into an electrical outlet. Neither act was repeated.

Our young twin son, after much soul searching and cautious deliberation, finally getting up the nerve to shyly ask his aunt, "Could I see you take out your teeth again?" Not only did she oblige but presented him with a no longer used set. That was when I started gritting my own.

Our other 4-year-old twin son, looking into our anxious eyes after his tonsillectomy, smiled and calmly asked for crackers and cheese. Our 7-year-old daughter, after her tonsillectomy, screaming that she was going to die, but wanted her ice cream first.

Discovering that our twin son, a possible future con artist, could sell peanuts to Jimmy Carter if he so desired, and succeed in doing so.

Our eleven-year-old daughter declaring she was leaving home, and walking off with her sleeping bag; my husband, following her in his car, returned home with her in time for dinner. The "nobody loves me" syndrome strikes again.

Losing my younger daughter in a department store, and breaking into tears when she appeared in the arms of a policeman, smiling and saying, "Hi Mommy!"

Reading our fourteen-year-old daughter's theme paper on puberty, noting the very descriptive phrases, and wondering where she learned all that stuff. It contained more than I will ever know.

Thinking that if all the chicken pox, measles, mumps and other ills, along with a broken arm, a broken collar bone and a hot appendix, were laid end to end, they would fade into nothing overshadowed by the realization that nothing compares to the feeling of pride when one can show to the world four children with four Masters degrees and four direct and frequent telephone lines to their parents.

Lastly, my husband presenting me with a ruby ring on our fortieth anniversary, and our children presenting us with a surprise party, attended by our favorite friends, making all the blood, sweat and tears disappear and the years seem more golden than a morning sunrise.

Where Did I Go Wrong?

Some of you know that I have produced (with a little help from my husband) a total of four children, with the hope that one day they will all become self-supporting. Naturally I thought their means of livelihood would probably be something glamorous like medicine, or law, or banking, or stardom, or the Presidency—things like that. To say that I had been living in Fantasyland would be an understatement. Let me say here, however, that I am proud and will forever be proud of the four of them and their accomplishments, even though there are a few times when I am unable to relate to these callings, impressive as they may be.

My oldest child, a daughter, is an ordained minister and co-pastor of her church in New York. Having been raised a Catholic, with three aunts who were nuns and an uncle who was a priest, I am at a loss to explain what happened. I can only conclude that having an audience with the Pope was never high on my daughter's list of priorities, or that religion, like politics, is all a matter of opinion—I think.

My younger daughter is a teacher of English as a second language. She has three textbooks to her credit, which is no mean feat. Since patience is not one of my many virtues, and certainly a definite requisite for this type of

36

career, I am afraid that if I were to be given a class of children to enlighten, there would be a group of bruised and battered young ones on the classroom floor at the sound of the closing bell. The number of irate parents who would suddenly appear as a result of this fiasco would make the *Guinness Book of Records*.

The first half of our set of twins (4 minutes older than his brother) works in something called Intellectual Properties. The only intellectual property I ever knew of is Albert Einstein, or maybe William F. Buckley, Jr. My son has very quietly explained that it has something to do with inventions. Why don't they say so? Since I have never been able to invent a good excuse for not putting dinner on the table, think what a miracle it would be for me to come up with a remote control window washer. And if you think I could, you might also believe that Mel Gibson and I are seeing each other on a regular basis.

My second son is a chemical engineer and owns his own business, which professed to be something having to do with pumps. These products are a far cry from the gadget that puts air in bicycle tires. Now I don't want to demean this worthy occupation, but I have been disappointed to learn that his considerable talents do not include plumbing repairs which may become necessary at this mother's house.

While none of my children have embarked upon a life work in television or appliance repair, or carpet cleaning or lawn maintenance, I can only assume that this represents a certain amount of wisdom on their part, allowing them to proceed with their own lives, blissfully aware that relating the relation are far removed from each other. Bless their little hearts.

DIVERSIONARY MENTIONABLES

The Only Game in Town

The following conversation took place in the office of the well-known divorce attorney, B. A. Freeman:

Mr. Freeman: Why on earth would you want to divorce your wife after twenty years, Mr. Cross?

Mr. Cross: She trumped my ace.

Of all the games devised by well-meaning people for the purpose of relaxation, challenge, mind sharpening, mind boggling, personal triumph and just pure enjoyment, the game of Bridge can be the deadliest.

Fortunes, friendships and reputations have been ruined by a mere deck of cards. The word "bridge" can mean something too far, or over the River Kwai, or something falling down in London, or an arch to raise the strings of a violin, or a replacement for lost teeth, but none can wreak havoc like what can go on when these 52 cards are dealt.

My mother was a bridge player and a master-pointer. A master-pointer is someone you don't argue with in front of anyone. She was a fan of Eli Culbertson for years. Since then many experts have tried to teach us about smart plays, both in bidding and playing. The latest is Omar Sharif, and while we may not agree with his methods, we can take heart by thinking about his handsome face and his role in "Dr. Zhivago."

Our Club offers the following opportunities:

Monday afternoon—Social—On this day you will be furnished with a partner who will be responsible for your arriving back home with either a good feeling or a headache.

Tuesday afternoon—Duplicate—You come with your own partner. This is the game where everyone is given the same hand to bid or play as the case may be. The object of this competetive endeavor is to see who makes the most points with the cards at hand. Even if you are given a lousy hand you can still win a prize by just sitting there and passing, even though you would rather be at the movies or shopping for a new outfit.

Thursday afternoon—Ditto Friday afternoon—Ditto Thursday evening—Member Club Bridge—Whatever it is, it is limited to Club members.

Then we have the Marathon Bridge for either couples or just women who play together. This includes a certain number of couples who dance from one home to another, each taking turns as host or hostess, with a grand finale at the end of the season. This usually includes dinner and the awarding of prizes, where no one is accused of cheating, at least not out loud.

There are ways of cheating, of course. You can ignore the talents of our bridge experts by such methods as pulling your ear, arranging your hair, putting your finger up your nose, by deep sighing or by smiling or frowning as the case may be.

If there is a woman in this Club who takes advantage of all these opportunities to play the game, she either lives alone or has a husband who enjoys a satisfying hobby which consumes all of his afternoons and some of his evenings, or plays golf.

Whatever your reasons for joining the ranks of those who play this game I hope you enjoy it as much as my mother did. She sat me down at the age of 12 to learn some Auction, and later Contract bridge. This was many years ago and I still don't know what I am doing. Believe me, I am much happier this way.

Count Me In!

Life has its ups and downs. Every cloud has a silver lining. Here today, gone tomorrow. Etc., etc., and blah, blah. You know them all. It happens to all of us, but in the heart of a gambler, there is no other way to live.

Just about every person on this earth has the urge to gamble. If you've ever bought a raffle ticket giving you a chance to win a million dollars, you are a gambler. If you have ever bet on a football game or joined a baseball pool, put a nickel in a candy machine with fake watches and jewelry, or drawn to an inside straight, you are a gambler.

If you have ever played bingo or pulled down the arm of a slot machine, or bought a ticket to win, place or show at a horse race, you are a gambler. If you have ever entered a sweepstakes contest, or filled out a form, hoping you'll win a trip to Hawaii, and placed it through a slot and into a box, you are a cheap gambler, but a gambler nevertheless.

My mother had the soul of a gambler. When I was born, she took one look at me and said, "Well, you win some, you lose some." A real sport, my mother. She had seven children, her lucky number. She would seat us around the dining room table and teach us to play every game there was. We mastered pig, hearts, rummy, fan tan, monopoly, Michigan, bridge, poker and a dozen more. She loved bingo. She gambled in the real estate market and won more than once. As a child, she would climb out of her bedroom window just to chase a fire in the night.

41

When she was a young woman, she managed to be engaged to two men at the same time. Now *that's* gambling. I am my mother's child. As long as there is a sporting chance, I will take it. My heart goes out to the cautious individual who treads the straight and narrow, who never wins, never loses. Such people really don't need my sympathy. They are quite content, and it is not necessary for them to experience the fear of losing or the joy of winning in order to lead a full life. They will never know the uncertainty of being on a waiting list.

I will not dwell on the greedy gambler who, already having won on "Let's Make A Deal" a refrigerator, stereo system and a mink coat, will sacrifice all just to see what lies behind the third door. Or the compulsive gambler, whose sickness affects his job, his home and his family. He is a born loser.

So, my fellow wagers and wagerettes, let us continue to make our yearly visit to Vegas for the fun of it. Let us pin our faith and financial hopes on the Wolverines and Lions and Tigers. Let us taste that queer-looking dish we've never had before, or investigate that small town off the beaten path we've never visited before. In other words, let's break the monotony of what otherwise could be a boring existence in this remarkable world.

Read Any Good Books Lately?

The little Putnam Township Library in Pinckney is the most favorite stop for me on my weekly errands. Not only do they carry most of the books on the best-seller list, but there is little or no waiting at all for these gems. Fortunately for me, the library uses the rather old-fashioned method of dispensing the books, wherein you sign your name to a small card which is in an envelope on the inside cover, which card is filed away in a box resembling something to contain shoes. Since I read at least four books within a week or ten-day period, I must on occasion glance at this card to find my signature before drawing out the book, just to make sure I haven't already read it, thus making my powers of memory a poor source of pride.

My choice of books is limited to the fictional, with an occasional autobiography thrown in. Most of the time these biographies so closely resemble a novel that I am inclined to pass them off as something not to be believed, whether the writer has had a political or cinematic or whatever career. The fictional offering, however, contains no such deceptions. It frankly admits that it is a novel, and that it is a product of the author's imagination, with no reference to any persons, living or dead, etc. It therefore becomes a pleasure for me to lay down the newspaper or magazine containing the sordid tales of everyday happenings in the real world, and to transport myself into the magical world of the yarn, the mystery, the romance and the suspense. But I have one little gripe.

As much as I enjoy reading every author from Barbara Cartland to Thomas Wolfe, I am appalled at the lack of imagination of some, but not all, of these writers when they describe their heroes or heroines with stereotyped phrases, especially if they are turning out their stories at a rapid rate.

The heroines invariably will have hair the color of spun gold, with eyes of violet or azure blue, a heart-shaped face that could be considered no less than beautiful, sitting atop a figure which would put any one of Charlie's Angels to shame. Or she would be tall and willowy, with raven hair, limpid brown eyes, and would never know

43

how seductive she really is. Then there is a flaming red-head with the snapping emerald eyes and a shape with more curves than the Columbia River Highway through the Rockies, and though she is temperamental, she is also quiet, refined and compassionate.

Now our hero is always tall—always. He has Nordic blond hair with ice blue eyes that thaw whenever he smiles at our heroine with his array of perfect white teeth, or he is handsome, with wavy dark hair, and wonder of wonders, gray eyes. Now I am a fool for gray eyes, and since I have seen only one pair in the last 40 years, I sometimes feel I am on this earth for the sole purpose of searching out another pair.

What percentage of women who read these romances can favorably compare these male gods with a husband who is short, bald, or who snores or is overweight?

What would happen if the Harlequin assembly line would roll out a novel wherein the hero was another Karl Malden who, in the rare times he removes his hat, would display on odd-looking toupee, but who turns out to be the world's greatest lover? Or the heroine who is 6′ 2″ tall, wearing glasses, who has allergies and sneezes a lot, but whose personality gathers men as honey gathers flies?

I'll tell you what would happen. Sales would take a dive and the publisher would jump out the nearest window. Realities seem to have no place in a novel. Such revelations would be too true to be good. Besides, who needs a fantasy trip like that?

Heaven in Your Hand

Whenever I tire of mysteries, biographical novels, science fiction, or what I like to call "heavy reading," I put my mind to rest and bring home, from the library, books guaranteed to produce good, clean fun, each book being known as the Regency Romance.

The Regency Romance is considered light reading, and though it will never win a Pulitzer Prize, it is guaranteed to rid your mind of stress, tension and worry as to how the story will end. The time is usually during the Victorian era, with the Prince Regent, sometimes known as "Prinny," making an appearance somewhere along the way. The setting is England and the plot will take you to cities such as London, Bath, Brighton or Oxford, or any other town or hamlet the author cares to mention.

Our hero is always, and I mean *always*, an Earl, a Duke, a Lord or a Marquis, or some other titled gentleman, who is tall, beautifully built, wealthy, and about as masculine as they come. He has eyes that twinkle, a smile that lights up the world, a magnificent sense of humor and a brain equal to that of Einstein. He is an athlete, a rascal, a gambler, a great lover, and he can spot a villain a mile away.

Our heroine can be attractive or downright stunningly beautiful. She can be short or tall and is possessed of hair any starlet would envy. She comes from acceptable stock and can be anything from a governess to the daughter of one who is addressed as "Sir" or "My Lord." She can be sassy, bewitching, sensible, fetching, maddening or headstrong, but above all, she is chaste, and would never indulge in any hanky panky.

The stories take you to routs and balls, to Almack's and Vauxhall Gardens, or to a season in London while describing in detail what everyone wears from head to toe. Our heroine is always the most sought after by her adoring swains, and our hero is always the most sought after by mothers of marriageable daughters, to no avail, of course. It is not a romantic courtship but a battle of wits, tempers, quarrels and misunderstandings between our two stars, but the ending is always the same, when love finally triumphs on the last page, so you really don't need to peek.

Some of us, in order to escape from the troubles of our lives or the sordid news we read every day, will turn to a situation comedy to enjoy a good laugh. And so will I, but reading these books of another era, another life style and another morality are no less than enjoyable, even if they stretch the truth and seem like fantasies.

These literary gems contain no sex scenes, no four-letter words, no murders, no violence beyond an honorable duel, no junkies, no police force, and no Rambos or Conans. So if this type of diversion doesn't appeal to you, go back to reading the daily news, or wallow in political corruption, or watch the cops and robbers on the idiot box, or wade through the afternoon soaps.

Enough already. Demean my intelligence if you will, but give me, please, a few hours of my day to fill my mind with stories of an unheard of Utopia, fill my heart with laughter and bring my tears for what could happen here, but never will.

The Old Age of Television

We have always referred to our television set as "Early LBJ." Sitting in front of this magnificent box, I toasted Mickey Lolich and the entire Detroit Tigers team when they won the pennant in 1968, or whenever. Since I am a TV idiot, I seldom missed *I Love Lucy* and the *Dick Van Dyke Show* and all the other sitcoms as well as the tear-jerkers and the cops and robbers fare. In the first six years, LBJ made one trip to the repair shop, a better than average record. We then transported him to Base Lake where, for three years and one more trip to the shop it was used only on weekends.

After three years we moved to Base Lake and hunted around for a regular TV repair man. We finally found one in the person of a man I shall call Dave. Dave was young and energetic when he made his first call.

As the years passed, Johnny Carson's hair became grayer, while J. R. Ewing's hair was slowly turning wavy, and Juliet Prowse's legs became fatter and she became shorter. During this period Dave seemed to age and his walk became slower each time he came to the house. One time he brought his son. Since he looked rather tired, I asked the boy, "Is your father well?" He replied that he thought that our LBJ was demoralizing his dad and could be responsible for those gray hairs popping out all over his head.

Soon one inch of action disappeared from the top and bottom of our picture. Then, after a period where we could see lovely colored horizontal lines and nothing more, we called again. Dave put us off for four days before dragging himself through the front door. We were happy to see him even though the feeling was not exactly mutual.

After a heated discussion, we decided it was time for a new set. Dave agreed to haul out LBJ if we couldn't find a buyer for it at our garage sale the following weekend. His parting shot was, "If you do happen to sell it to some guy, please don't tell him where I am."

Our garage sale came and went, during which time we managed to bid our set a fond good-bye. A few days later my husband walked into Dave's shop and said, "I have some good news and some bad news. The good news is that we sold LBJ, and the bad news is . . . . "

We have a new set now, but whether we still have Dave is anybody's guess.

47

RHYME TIME

Medical Progress?

This article was taken from Ann Landers' column in the *Ann Arbor News* Thursday, December 9, 1990:
To quote: "And now I read about yet another remarkable effort. Scientists have now made it possible for women who have gone through menopause to become pregnant through the implantation of 'donated' eggs.

Cut it out, you folks in the nation's research centers. There is still a long list of diseases we have no cure for. Please work on them and don't "help" women in their late 40s and 50s have babies. The best break Mother Nature gives us is menopause and the freedom from pregnancy. Please, geniuses, keep your cotton-pickin' hands off this God-given blessing."

Right On, Sister
Oh! Donate not your eggs to me
Whose age is more than fifty-three
A baby now would only be
A blow to my fertility.
I've been too long relaxed and free
To welcome this calamity
So close to my senility,
From donor's eggs—deliver me!

Feminized Asparagus Spurs Suits

From the Associated Press:

Newark, N.J.—A commercial nursery charges that Rutgers University feminized an all-male breed of asparagus and then blamed the nursery for the inadvertent sex change.

Rutgers sued Nourse Farms last month. In a countersuit filed Wednesday in federal court, the nursery charged New Jersey's largest university with fraud, slander, misappropriation of research funds and trying to destroy its business, among other allegations.

The University said Thursday it stands by the allegations in its lawsuit. Officials declined further comment.

Both sides were to appear before U. S. District Judge John Bissell today.

The nursery in South Deerfield, Mass., was responsible for reproducing a super all-male seed called the Jersey Giant, which Rutgers developed.

The macho hybrid produces only male asparagus seed, which can yield up to four times as many vegetables as a sexually mixed crop, no small feat in a country that eats almost 245 million pounds of asparagus a year.

In 1985, however, feminine genes contaminated the super male seeds, and it wasn't until 1989 that they regained their all-male characteristics. In July, 1990, the feminine contamination returned.

In the newest suit, Nourse blames Rutgers and asks for unspecified compensatory and punitive damages.

Shame on the nasty farms who raise asparagus!
When will they stop attempting to disparage us?
Resulting from their chauvinist perversity
A host of lawsuits plague the university

For bringing macho hybrid to its knees
By changing its new crop from "hes" to "shes".
Hurrah! I say to women who hold high
Their spear and cheer their victory. My! My!

Wearin' Go Bragh

This is a reflection brought about by the news of the latest invention from Japan of a remarkable new bra, which when fastened on and worn by the female of the species, will play a selection from Mozart.

Blessings on the Japanese
Whose claim to fame has been to please
The buying public with inventions
For the young and those on pensions.
Now Mozart plays inside our bra
His rendering of la-de-da.
While younger girls might want instead
Some music from the Grateful Dead,
The older matron would prefer
A chorus of The Way We Were.

I'M GLAD YOU ASKED

Let Maggie Help You

Dear Maggie,

My boyfriend is thirty years old. He is tall, blond and quite good looking. He has given me very expensive gifts and takes me everywhere. He is quite charming and I like him a lot. His father is wealthy but his mother talks about nothing but horses and I couldn't live with that. What can I do to shake him off?

Lonely in Lexington

Dear Lonely,

I'll tell you what you can do—you can send me his name, address and phone number. Rest assured, you will not hear from him again. Tally-ho!

Dear Maggie,

I am eleven years old. I sent my grandmother a shawl for her birthday. She wrote back to thank me and said she was going to wear it over her bikini when she goes to the beach for her surfing lesson. Are all grandmothers like that?

Angie in Indiana

Dear Angie,

All grandmothers are not like that. The ones I know would probably wear a short lace jacket over their bikinis. They're more in style. Your grandmother should wake up to what's in and what's out at the beach.

Dear Maggie,

I am a forty-five-year-old man. I had admitted my age to my friends and my sister is furious with me. The problem is that she is my twin and has told everyone she is only thirty-eight. She has threatened to shoot me. What shall I do?

Scared in Scarsdale

Dear Scared,

After buying a bullet-proof vest and hiring a bodyguard, you should resort to prayer. Even without breaking a mirror you have already asked for seven years worth of bad luck.

Dear Maggie,

My boyfriend and I go out to dinner occasionally. However, when we are riding home in the car, he sometimes picks his teeth. Should I object to this?

Fussy in Findlay

Dear Fussy,

Not as long as he keeps them in his mouth.

Dear Maggie,

Who do you think has the greatest legs in the world?

Grampa in Tampa

Dear Grampa,

My former husband. I am still trying to catch up with him and my back alimony checks.

Dear Maggie,

I am a member of the opposite sex and I don't think you are being fair to either one of us. The answers you give are too biased for me to understand your slanted opinions. Why don't you straighten up your act?

Furious in Philly

Dear Furious,

Do you want to run that one by me again?

Dear Maggie,

I am a secretary making $300.00 a week. When I received my weekly pay check last Friday I was surprised to find it was in the amount of $675,729.25. The temptation to cash it is so great. What should I do?

Weakening in Wichita

Dear Weakening,

Nincomputers are never wrong. They are also never right. Return the check and your honesty will be rewarded just as sure as I will be having dinner with Burt Reynolds tonight.

Dear Maggie,

My husband, who is a chef, is having an affair with another woman. When I complained about this he only laughed and said not to worry. She was only interested in him because she enjoyed his cooking. There must be a name for someone like her.

Steaming in Saline

Dear Steaming,

There is. She is what you call a side dish.

When in Mexico

If you are given a traffic ticket, you can elect to receive a police escort to the station to pay your fine, and if you are lucky you will get back your driver's license.

If you are a blonde or a redhead and are visiting Mexico, the males will appear out of the pyramids and lay out the red carpet for you. If you are a parent, some enterprising young Mexican will offer to buy your fair-haired daughter for pesos. Think about it.

If there is some soap missing from your hotel room and you think you are being smart by asking the cleaning woman for "soap-a," she will bring you a bowl of soup. Good, too.

If your gas tank or muffler seem to be about to depart your car, almost any mechanic can repair it with a coat hanger. Be sure to carry one with you.

If your cab driver takes off at a high rate of speed after depositing you at the train station, the Federales could pick him up and escort him to your compartment on the train to make sure you were not overcharged for the taxi trip. If you are smart you will say the fare was okay, unless you would like a visit to the police station to testify, thereby missing your train.

Your dentist, even if he is not bi-lingual, knows three English words: "Open de mowf." If he wants to tell you something or ask you something, he will pick up the phone which is convenient to his drilling station, call and talk to a fellow dentist who speaks English. Then he will hand you the phone so you can receive the English translation which sometimes begins with "Is he hurting you?" and ends with "Your dentist would like a deposit of...."

If you come out of your hotel room some morning and note that your car looks clean and shiny, chances are there will be a small boy standing beside it with a rag in his hand. Be sure to thank him with a few pesos.

If a train in Mexico stops or breaks down along the way, you are at liberty to wait until the problem is solved or you may elect to pick up your luggage, find the nearest road and flag down the first bus. This could be a second class vehicle, in which case you could find yourself sharing your seat with either an animal or a human. Don't complain. The bus will get you there, hopefully.

One evening in Morelia at the Villa Montana we watched (with a doctor friend) from the balcony overlooking the city, the view of the cathedral bathed in a sea of light, a beautiful picture. Our friend, wanting a picture of the sight, set up his tripod and camera the next evening in order to take home this memento. Imagine his disappointment when the lights refused to come on. We subsequently learned this occasion occurred only twice a year, on Christmas and on the birthday of Benito Juarez. Watch out for Benito. He could spoil your whole trip.

Mexico can be fun, especially if your name is "Marguerita."

The E.R.A. Handbook for Homemakers

You are married. You have a husband, maybe some children. You live in a house on a street. You do not rise each day, toss off some orange juice and coffee and dash off to some glamorous employment in a corporate office or a noodle factory, with never a backward glance at the imaginary iron bars on the windows and doors of your home. Instead, you prefer to remain where you are, regard yourself as a homemaker, with nary a dream in your heart to be part of the struggle of the masses in the cruel world outside.

However, with the potential power of the Equal Rights Amendment becoming more noticeable, and its invasion into every woman's world with the force of the French Revolution a distinct possibility, you decide to give the matter some thought.

Are you really free? Of course you are. You're free to do the housework in your underwear if you like, you can do the laundry any day you please, and if you don't like liver you can cook whatever you want for dinner. And you don't have to take the same route when you drive the kids to dancing school, or the dentist, or whatever. And so on. Now that's freedom!

Now let's look at the working woman. Is she really free? Of course she is. She's free to show up at work anytime before the doors open and she's free to leave anytime after the doors close. And if she doesn't feel like working she's free to look for another job. Or if her salary is 59% of her male counterpart's she's free to go home and sulk. After hours, of course.

With just these few examples as a guide, you decide you like it the way it is, but you still want to create the impression that you are not some lowly housewife without an intelligent brain in her head. So here are a few helpful suggestions to assist you in making that impression:

A business associate calls your husband, who is in the shower, and you answer the phone. In your best Sylvia Porter manner you say: "Could I have him return your call in about an hour? He's working himself into a lather trying to liquidate his assets. Let's hope everything doesn't go down the drain."

How about this one? You are having lunch at a fancy restaurant (you do get a day off, don't you?) with some of your homemaker friends. You announce that lunch is on you, because your husband has given you a raise (a bigger household allowance due to inflation). The conversation then goes something like this:
Friend: Raise? What raise?

You: I am referring to monetary value for goods and
    services rendered.
Friend: You get paid?
You: Doesn't everyone?

Or this one: At a cocktail party you have this repartee
with the man standing next to you:
You: I invested everything I had in silver today. (The
    flatware needed polishing.)
Friend: (real cute) I hope it doesn't tarnish your port-
    folio.
You: (cuter) Oh, I usually examine it from time to
    time.
Friend: (cutest) What a sterling idea!
You: I was only practicing. My mother warned me
    not to marry you.
He: You'll just have to clean up your act.

Well, you can't score every time, but if you don't watch
out, this kind of thing can happen on one of your bad
days:

You have a headache, your teenage son has taken
your car, your husband is bringing company to din-
ner, the house is a mess, and your sister-in-law is on
the phone hoping you will say a few kind words
about Phyllis Schaffly. You sigh and ask, "What is
she doing out on the road all the time when she
should be home showing all those women who are
out on the road all the time that they ought to be
at home?" And your sister-in-law replies, "Nobody's
perfect, darling. And don't forget your little goodies
for the bake sale on Saturday." Now is the time for
you to write that book about in-laws.

But if you are really smart, you'll go back to the beginning, because this is what it's all about, and you keep it to yourself, because it's beautiful.

You are newly married and expecting your first child. Whether you know it or not, there is no position of responsibility on this earth greater than what is soon to be yours. No power anywhere is stronger than what you hold when you take on the appalling task of presenting to the world another human being old enough and fit enough to live in your society.

THERE'LL ALWAYS BE A CHRISTMAS

Christmas in Mexico—1965—A True Story

From Mexico's Highway 15 the road leading to San Blas slowly descends from 3,500 feet to sea level, covering a distance of 23 miles. As the climate grows more tropical so does the foliage on either side of the road. Coconut palms, banana and papaya trees are visible everywhere. The quietude is disturbed occasionally by the song of the egret or the roseated spoonbill, then at last the road meanders out of this peaceful jungle into the busy town of San Blas.

Once the original West coast port of entry for imports to Mexico in a time when there was no Panama Canal, and ships sailed around South America, San Blas still retains its colonial charm. The old customs buildings and warehouses are slowly sinking into decay, while atop the hill overlooking the town the old fort stands with its cannons still in position, as if in constant guard against any adversary.

As I pulled up in front of the Hotel Playa Hermosa, I could almost hear the engine of our station wagon breathe a sigh of relief. It was December 21, 1965, and the day was a hot one. I was thinking that if Santa Claus visited San Blas this year, he had better be wearing a red T-shirt and shorts. My wife, Willie, (her real name is Mary) climbed out of the front seat and, grabbing one of the suitcases, hurried into the hotel to what she hoped would

61

be some kind of respite from the heat. The lobby was cooler, as was our room. Nice and comfortable, with a huge shower that I raced Mary to. She won.

Later, in the bar waiting for a couple of Margaritas, we took in the thatch-decorated walls, the heavy beams and the old-fashioned ceiling fans. Over in one corner was the band area. The bartender managed to get across to us with what English he knew that the big night in the hotel was Christmas Eve, when the *mariachis* would play in their special outfits—black velvet jackets with silver buttons, and fancy sombreros decorated in silver. We promised to be around.

It was cooler that evening so we walked over to the town square. There were a few people milling around so we latched onto a local resident whose name was Roger de Dios, and who just happened to be a vocalist with the town *mariachis*.

"Tomorrow," he said, "all the children will be here to try to hit *pinatas*. You can see now the rope from the church over to that lamp post. Here the *pinatas* will be hung and a man in the church will work the rope. Then the children will be blindfolded and with a stick will try to hit them so they will break and the candy will fall out. You can buy a *pinata* for them if you like."

"Let's buy one, Vince," said my dear wife.

"Okay, we'll do it tomorrow," I said.

The next afternoon, after a walk on the beach and a look-see at the town we showed up at the square with our pesos, ready to splurge on one of those papier-mache animals. There were chickens, burros and bunnies, among others. We settled on an owl with great big eyes and paid a whopping 40 cents, then discovered at the last minute that our owl had an empty stomach. Fine thing. So another 25 cents filled the bird with candy and the children went to work.

"Just call me El Cheapo," I said to Willie.

The guy standing next to me taking in the fun was a vegetable buyer from San Francisco. Name of Dillon. "It's cheaper for me to buy here and ship home by rail than to get produce from Florida," he said. "The workers here in the tomato and pepper fields are paid only $1.25 a day, barely enough to live on. However, nothing stops them from enjoying a fiesta at this time of year."

"What happens after the *pinatas?*" I asked.

"Nothing now until Christmas Eve, when the children will parade through the town with lighted candles, leading a donkey carrying the Virgin Mary, a young girl wearing a long white dress. It is very nice to watch. But the rest of the evening will be a disappointment to the children."

"How so?"

"Usually there are the fireworks after the parade, but the *padre* has told the little ones that there is no money to buy them this year."

After Dillon left, Willie and I sat on one of the benches and counted our pesos.

"See what you can do," she said.

She wandered around while I went to hunt up the *padre*. I found him in his small office in the church, and he told me what the fireworks would cost.

I pulled myself together and pressed the money into his hands. Managing a smile, I said, *"Para los ninos."* He thanked me and I left to find Mary.

On Christmas Eve we joined the townspeople to watch the parade. The singing of the children echoed through the streets, and the dark eyes in their tiny faces looked sort of starry in the light of the candles. Afterward there was a mad rush to the square to watch the fireworks. The ohs and ahs ran through the crowd as the glowing pinwheels and fiery designs mounted on their stands brightened the night. But that was only a prelude to the final gasp of surprise when Roger de Dios ran into the square. He was wearing a rattan "El Toro" over his head, from which some kind of sparklers lit up one after another. It made a great end to the evening for the kids.

Back at the hotel Willie and I headed for the bar, carrying our recorder, and taped the great music of the *mariachis*. We found out they had never made a record, so we played their music back for them. The broad grins on their faces as they listened to themselves made the whole thing worthwhile.

On Christmas Day we enjoyed the traditional turkey dinner and later began packing up to leave, almost sorry we had to go. It had been a different and enjoyable holiday for us and made us feel warm all over, not just from the weather outside.

At 8:00 a.m. the following morning we started back to Highway 15 on our way to Guadalajara. About an hour later Willie finally got around to asking the big question.

"How much did you have to pay for those fireworks, anyway?"

I told her.

"Fourteen dollars!" she screamed. "Is that all?"

"Yup," I said, "El Cheapo strikes again!"

Long Ago This Christmas

The old man and the small boy sat together on a park bench. It was December, and the air was crisp, but the wind was so still that the recent light fall of snow remained undisturbed except for the bootprints of those out for a stroll.

Although he was in his eighties, the old man's eyes were still as blue and clear as the sky above them, and his smile as bright as the sun which was now beginning to penetrate his woolen shawl to warm his tired shoulders and back. In his gloved hand he held his great-grandson's small, mittened one. Both were quiet for some time, then the boy spoke.

"Grandpa, what was Christmas like when you were a little boy?"

"Pretty much like it is now, I guess, except..."

"Except what, Grandpa?"

"Well, except that it seemed harder and easier, and smaller and bigger, and poorer and richer, and I think sadder and happier."

"That's silly!" said the boy.

The old man laughed. "It sounds silly, doesn't it? But cutting down a big tree and pulling it across a big field of snow was no simple task. Sometimes it took hours, but it seemed easier because it was what everyone had to do to get a tree, and we helped each other, and it was fun."

"What about smaller and bigger?"

"The bag Santa Claus carried was a lot smaller in those days, so the presents were fewer, but the congregation in our little chapel seemed bigger than it is in any church today."

"A lot of people go to church at Christmas, Grandpa. And I'm going to be a shepherd in our school play."

"Congratulations. But our little chapel was filled every Sunday, not just at Christmas. We were poorer, to be sure, and had very few possessions, but the wealth of our friendship and togetherness as we sang our carols seemed to make our voices richer than at any other time."

"Well, maybe Christmas was happier then, Grandpa, but why was it sadder?"

"Because in those days life seemed simpler and the world was less troubled. People didn't have so much to concern themselves with at this time of year, except that some felt sad to think that one small child born in a stable must grow up to give his life so that we could all love each other more." The blue eyes were misty now.

"Why are you crying, Grandpa? Are you sad because Christmas is coming?"

"Sad? No, indeed. These are happy tears because the angels are coming again and I am here and I have you to share my day." As he gazed down at the small, up-turned face, he silently offered a prayer of hope. Then, calling upon his biggest smile, he added, "I guess things really haven't changed so much after all."

No Christmas? Think About It.

What do you figure would happen if we didn't have
   Christmas at all?
Never to honor a birthday, never to deck the great hall.
Would the churches be dark and the store windows stark?

We would have no need for tinsel and no need for pop-
   corn to string,
We never would know of the Christ-child or the fun that
   our giving might bring,
And would "Joy to the World" be a banner still furled?

The tree would remain in the forest, there wouldn't be
   cards we might send,
We wouldn't have need of a punch bowl for egg nog to
   share with a friend.
Would the turkey still strut or our doors remain shut?

The North Pole would just be another small dot on the
world atlas map,
And children would never write Santa or sit on his
generous lap.
Would the reindeer not fly with the sleigh in the sky?

The blessings would never be counted by families on this
special day,
And laughter, excitement and pleasure could never have
happened this way.
Would the day be another just like any other?

And who would have thought a mere Christmas could
fill any dark day with light,
Could bring out the laughter of children or the memory
of one ''Silent Night''?
Yes, it surely is true—I'd concede, wouldn't you?

THE WILDER SIDE OF PROVIDENCE

The Wilder Side of Providence

The Almighty has answered many a prayer, and He answered one of mine many years ago, but in such a devastating way that I am almost afraid to plead for His help these days with any great degree of fervor, for fear of His accommodating me in a manner even approaching that of His past action in my behalf. Thinking about it, though, I don't remember being surprised or shocked at this particular method of His when it happened, only a quiet relief in having a soul-stirring weight lifted from the fragile shoulders of a nine-year-old girl, so that what was a reward for unswerving faith to me then, today impresses me as having been a huge calamity.

The Great Depression had not yet descended upon us the year my parents placed me in St. Mary's Academy for Girls at Monroe, Michigan. It's difficult for me to remember if I was sad or happy at this decision of theirs to do this, but I do remember growing to dislike the school as time moved along that first year. It disturbed me that my toothpaste was not the brand all of the other girls were using. My parents didn't visit me as often as other parents visited their daughters, and since I had been cursed with straight brown hair which had been styled in a Dutch bob with bangs constantly covering my eyes, it always looked horrible alongside the cute styles worn by the other girls. Then too, I usually ate the food placed before me at mealtime, since my parents had taught me to abhor waste, an attitude quite unlike my fellow students who regarded all convent food with disdain. Consequently, around the dining table I was considered something of a nut. These little things, added to the solid fact that my two aunts, Sister Verena and Mother Thomasina, were well known and highly esteemed nuns in the order of the Immaculate Heart of Mary, almost made my life unbearable. I know I was expected to be the epitome of good deportment, and any deviation from this behavior would immediately reflect upon my family and send all the nuns of this Academy into shock. I lived with my constant fear of the nuns, of displeasing them or of saying the wrong thing, not only at the wrong time but at any time.

Having suffered my way through the school year, wherein the only bright spot was the privilege of dancing the minuet along with the other girls before the older Henry Ford and Mrs. Ford (at the time my bangs were halfway down my nose, but the excitement of the evening far surpassed the embarrassment), I welcomed the warm sun of June with a glad feeling. Home was only two weeks away on the Sunday when my father came alone to visit me. We spent a busy day in the city, where I was allowed to consume every confection my eyes beheld, and it would have horrified me if anyone had attempted to spoil my day by telling me that I would be sick. But sick I was—and in the car on the way back to the convent. The whole front of my uniform was a mess!

Let me tell you about our uniforms. Our daily wear consisted of a navy blue serge creation with a sailor collar trimmed in narrow navy braid, and having a pleated skirt which stopped at mid-calf, showing medium brown cotton stockings and brown oxfords. The stockings were held up by a waist harness of some sort with attached adjustable garters. On Sundays we wore a black serge uniform with a round neck, to which was attached a washable small, white Peter Pan collar. This dress, too, had a pleated skirt the same length as the other, overlooking the same cotton stockings, but the shoes were black patent Mary Janes, requiring the services of a button hook for easy buckling. Both navy and black made my olive skin look drab and muddy. It was, of course, the Sunday garb that I had ruined that day, and I felt as if nothing more that was horrible could happen to me.

My father bought me some gingerale which seemed to settle my stomach to his satisfaction, then in a typically male maneuver, quickly dropped me off at the convent with the request that I see Sister Marcella about my uniform. Sister Marcella! I'd rather die first! Such a woman, even though a devoted godly nun, would never understand! Her pinched face would stare at me, and her unspoken words would pierce my very heart and strip me of all self-respect. No, no, I couldn't bear the shame of it!

I raced to the dormitory before anyone could see my dress, changed into my daily uniform, threw the soiled one into the closet, grabbed my black veil and rushed to the chapel to present myself for Sunday Vespers. Naturally my outfit did not go unnoticed. Sister Marcella gave me one of her looks, but miraculously did not question me about the change, then or later.

By now I had begun to pray. Seven days in which to do something about my Sunday dress! My prayers were not for strength or courage to speak to Sister Marcella. No amount of assistance could have given me that. No, they were much less complicated. They simply asked God to take away the old soiled uniform and put another in its place. Surely the good Lord would understand my position, my terror at the thought of speaking up, and most importantly, the short time before next Sunday would arrive. Of course He would. Even in my fright I knew He would take care of everything, and He did, but not in the manner I had prescribed for Him.

On Friday afternoon at three thirty the offensive uniform was still in my closet, so I was a little concerned as I went outside to play. The day was bright and sunny and somehow made me feel better inside as I joined my friends. We were skipping rope when we noticed a small stream of black smoke emerging from a basement window of the convent. This created a little excitement for a short time only, for none of us ever dreamed that anything could destroy this huge, magnificent academy constructed of solid brick with its many imposing turrets and wide cement steps leading to the front entrance, a structure even blessed by the Bishop at its time of completion and first enrollment. But we were wrong. The smoke became thicker and blacker, all pupils and nuns were removed from the building and the entire group of occupants was taken across the street to the old convent to watch and to wait.

It was a fantastically beautiful fire to watch, for it levelled this great piece of architecture right to the ground. Parents were called, and while we waited to be taken home (hoping to find something which might be ours) we rummaged through trinkets and personal belongings which the firemen brought to us at various intervals. Some of the younger girls (of which I was one) were crying, but I?—I was at peace. I did not even regret the loss of a beautiful new flowered bedspread and Italian doll my mother had recently brought me from Europe. They were so new I had not as yet developed any sort of attachment to them. My mind winced a little at the loss of the doll (I knew the spread was done for good), but when the firemen failed to rescue it, I accepted the loss with a small proud feeling of maturity.

Later, when the tears did come, they were tears of anger, for my mother was one of the very last to arrive, and I had no desire to remain the night in the old convent. When she did come the tears disappeared and I happily climbed into the car. I slept on the way home. It was a good sleep, with no bad dreams of saintly Sister Marcella standing beside the fire chief and holding up a black Sunday uniform for all the world to see.

C O L O P H O N

This book is one of an edition of
six hundred fifty copies
printed and bound at The Golden Quill Press,
in the year nineteen-hundred ninety-two.
The text is set in a digital facsimile
of a typeface designed in 1540 by
Geofroy Tory's pupil, Claude Garamond,
on command of Francois I of France.
The text paper, Smyth-sewn in sixteen page signatures,
is Mohawk Mills' sixty-pound basis acid-free
Mohawk Cream White Vellum, manufactured at
Cohoes, New York.

This infinity symbol ∞
represents Golden Quill's commitment to quality paper stock,
which will last several centuries,
and our cooperation with
The National Information Standards Organization, Washington, DC.